D0726249

Penguins

Julie Murray

Abdo
I LIKE ANIMALS!
Kids

abdopublishing.com

Published by Abdo Kids, a division of ABDO, PO Box 398166, Minneapolis, Minnesota 55439.
Copyright © 2017 by Abdo Consulting Group, Inc. International copyrights reserved in all countries.
No part of this book may be reproduced in any form without written permission from the publisher.

Printed in the United States of America, North Mankato, Minnesota.

102016

012017

THIS BOOK CONTAINS
RECYCLED MATERIALS

Photo Credits: iStock, Shutterstock

Production Contributors: Teddy Borth, Jennie Forsberg, Grace Hansen

Design Contributors: Christina Doffing, Candice Keimig, Dorothy Toth

Publisher's Cataloging in Publication Data

Names: Murray, Julie, author.

Title: Penguins / by Julie Murray.

Description: Minneapolis, Minnesota : Abdo Kids, 2017 | Series: I like animals! |
      Includes bibliographical references and index.

Identifiers: LCCN 2016943919 | ISBN 9781680809077 (lib. bdg.) |
      ISBN 9781680796179 (ebook) | ISBN 9781680796841 (Read-to-me ebook)

Subjects: LCSH: Penguins--Juvenile literature.

Classification: DDC 598.47--dc23

LC record available at http://lccn.loc.gov/2016943919

Table of Contents

Penguins

Penguins are birds.

But they do not fly.

They have feathers. They are
black and white.

They **waddle**. Their legs are short.

Their feet are webbed. They have flippers.

They can swim fast!

Sharp beaks help them catch food.

They eat small fish.

They also eat krill.

They live in large groups.

They stay close to keep warm.

Have you seen a penguin?

Some Kinds of Penguins

Adélie penguin

king penguin

emperor penguin

macaroni penguin

Glossary

waddle
to walk with short steps,
rocking from side to side.

flipper
a wide flat limb that helps
with swimming.

webbed
having toes connected by
skin tissue.

Index

abdokids.com

Use this code to log on to abdokids.com and access crafts, games, videos, and more!

Abdo Kids Code:
IPK9077